THE WALL
AND OTHER POEMS

For information address

J2B Publishing LLC
4251 Columbia Park Road
Pomfret, MD 20657
www.J2BLLC.com
GladToDoIt@gmail.com

Cover Photo: Adirondack Back Range by Benjamin Yates Brewster Jr.
Printed and bound in the United States of America

IBSN: 978-1-948747-63-9

THE WALL
AND OTHER POEMS

Richard I. Gold

J2B Publishing

Also by Richard I. Gold

Dedication

My thanks for the support of my wife and to those who have reviewed these poems and made valuable suggestions.

Table of Contents

THE WALL

Walls are made of stone and wood
Designed to keep intruders out
They stand firm in place
When an attack others mount

But there are other walls
Not made of solid stone
They are of custom and law
Make us hold our own

There are legal walls
Which the system stock
They are just as real
As those made of rock

But for each wall
There is a way to go
To allow an opening
To those who are in the know

In the wall that confronts me
There is a triumphal arch
If I but had eyes to see
Through it I could march

IT IS ODD

It is odd
From birth until we're beneath the sod
The many things we seek
Are the chains that do us keep

To seek what is good
To seek what is right
Makes us what we ought to be
Makes our future bright

We cannot change the fact
But only choose our goal
For if the good chains we take
The holding will make us whole

I SIT UPON THE BRINK

I sit upon the brink of life
I dare not be too bold
But when I take the plunge
The future I will hold

The future is a murky place
With many dangers wrought
It is a place where we must go
Souls to be sold and bought

But with each danger comes opportunities
With each test a hope
We must be prepared
To always be able to cope

To prepare for the future
To be all that we can be
Then by our guiding light
The golden hope we will see

TO LOVE AND LOSE

To love and to lose
Is not what we desire
Sometimes what we have lost
Is worse than a fire

A fire burns the skin
The flesh it does devour
Sets the body in pain
An everlasting fire

But the loss of love
Burns the very soul
It takes more than time
To make the person whole

SNOW

For those who live in colder climes
Those who must travel out
There is a word the clogs the mind
Really has great clout

What is that word?
It is as every driver does know
That word gives us chills
That word is snow

It clogs the roads
It clogs the walks
It stops the world
All we can do is talk

How do we remove this bane?
It takes the breaking back
We shovel it to one side
Exercise we so not lack

But believing in use of nature
Is where we should run
That to remove the snow
We rely on nature's sun

PLEASING TO GOD

Would you be pleasing to God?
And to your fellow man?
Follow the twelve commandments
That were set by His Holy Hand

The Bible has a list of ten
The law of the blest
But there are two others
That summarize the rest

The Ten Commandments starts
With a statements of who God is
The one who freed the slaves
And called them to be His

The two other commandments
That summarize all the rest
Is the love only God
Let your love stand the test

The other commandment
Is how to treat others
To love them as ourselves
Treat them like brothers

HAVE YOU HEARD

Have you heard?
Heard the word
The word of love
Love from above

Above the word you've heard
Above the madding crowd
We hear thoughts of love
To our soul shouted loud

So love your lover
With a love so pure
And your lover will love you
With a love that will endure

THE SKY IS MY ROOF

The sky is my roof
My floor is the ground
My walls are tall and green
Trees and grass all around

The wander goes walking
Through the world of toil and sin
When this one returns
He knows where he has been

Those who walk the world
Much experience do gain
But unless they use wisely
It will be in vain

WHEN YOU'RE YOUNG

When you're young
The world is your cherry
You like to go out
You like to make merry

When you're a little older
You begin to understand
You did what you did
But should have a reprimand

As you grow into an adult
You acquire responsibility
Understand the bridges burned
Have become a liability

By the time you become older
Your life is more sedate
Your younger ways
You begin to hate

All in all it is your life
You have lived in a crunch
Pay your money and take your chances
But you only live once

LIFE IS SHORT

Life is short
As short as it can be
It seems it is over
Before we start to see

But if the sage is right
What he says is true
Life is forever
About that we can have nothing to do

How we live forever
Will depend upon us now
What we think and believe
What we say and how

THE VALUE OF HUMAN LIFE

We all desire to live
Our days to the end
In the race of life
To be able to win

To live in a society
Requires us to make a contribution
For those who take, not give
We should require retribution

Long days and joyous
Will make life worth while
Give a reason to live
Beats the alternative by a mile

It is a human dictum
That we get as we give
So the human life we save
Will help us to live

The value of a human life
Whether mine, yours or theirs
Is written on the human soul
Given in our prayers

For life is a sacred trust
We receive from God
If we take another
Our soul will remain in the sod

VOLUNTEER

We often work for others
Without any pay
We wish to help out
Aid them every day

We do it for the pay they give
It is not in money but in words true
That by their life, and in their hope
They just say "Thank you"

"Thank you" means so much
It really shows they care
And helps us when we sacrifice
To go and be there

WHEN THE WIND

When the wind
Whistles through the trees
When the sun
Sets upon the lake

When the birds
Sing songs of spring
When lovers walk
In the sunset lane

I will sing
Love songs to thee
It will give
Marvelous things from me

So be my love
And I'll be yours
We'll sing together
Through many years

HOW WOULD YOU BE REMEMBERED?

How would you be remembered?
What would have them say?
When you are no longer here
On your funeral day

We do many things
That we know are right
That we live each day
Through the dark, dark night

There are many things
That I would have of them
"In life he loved
In death we love him"

WHAT WOULD YOU OWN?

What would you own?
That your happiness would insure
Is it the things
Or experiences to endure

The most prized to own
If the future that you have
To know what you should do
To know what needs to save

Would you own the future?
Would you make it your own?
Prepare for what may come
Preparation will take you home

THE FUTURE

The future is a blank page
With events both bad and good
We would that we did know
To do what we should

The future can be a pain
If we do not have a plan
If we choose to do nothing
Our foundation will be sand

The future is an opportunity
Of which we should take
For whether profit or loss
It is ours to make

MONEY

Money
Like many things in life
Is sets us going
It gets us what we want
Keeps our influence growing

But money is a fragile thing
With which to measure wealth
It can give us worry
Cost us our health

Come inflation
When a dollar is worth a dime
When all our savings
Are not worth the time

As long as we make ends meet
Keep a roof over our head
Be happy and help others
The future we shall not dread

WHERE THE SKY MEETS THE SEA

Where the ocean is flat
Where the sky is so blue
There I sit
There I think of you

I sit and I look
Where the sky meets the sea
I know somewhere
You are waiting for me

My love is devoted
So tenderly to you
If only we could talk
I'd tell you I'm true

So wait for me my love
Love me so dear
For I'll be back to you
By this time next year

LOVE IS A DEVELOPING THEME

Love is a developing theme
A state to which you have to work
If you should ever lose
Your duty you will shirk

But life is given
Like a personal gift
It is not taken
It is not caused by a rift

Love is an emotion
Straight from the heart
But for love to begin
You must do your part

To make love grow
There is no letting down
Keep working at it
Make the base sound

Love pays great dividends
To those who find it true
It lives for all our lives
When others think of you

SLEEPING ON THE JOB

Sleeping is a part of life
An important part of the day
There's a time and place for it
But there are places it doesn't pay

The job at which we work
At which we spend our time
Is the goal of our life
Part of our prime

Sleeping on the job
Is neither good nor right
If you have extra time
You might lose your job, you might

AS I LAY SLEEPING

As I lay sleeping
In my bed so dear
I heard a purring
In my ear

It is a dream and nothing more

The louder it grew
The more I was awakened
The paws on my leg
My sleep was shaken

It is a dream and nothing more

Across my back
To my ear
There goes my sleep
My sleep so dear

Out the door and nothing more

CATS

Cats, cats, cats, cats
I have cats that live with me
They beg for attention and food
And drive me up a tree

There is nothing like a cat
To warm the cockles of the heart
For they are like babies
And we must do our part

But ere I love them
And treat them as my own
They show they love me
And call my house their home

FOUR CATS

I have four cats
Four cats have me
But sometimes I wish
It was four cats minus three

They are warm and furry
Their love is quite a bane
Their personalities are all different
But do they have a brain?

But it is nice to have them
Their fur is soft as a dove
And when I feed them
Their undivided love

CATS ARE ALL DIFFERENT

Cats are all different
Yet they are the same
They live in a world of their own
Sometimes answer to their name

All cats want to be the only one
Their world not to share
They'll give to other cats
As long as they are not there

To your cat
You are their mother
They look to you for what they want
And to no one other

IN DAYS OF OLD

In days of old
Knights were bold
And women were so becoming
The battles they fought
With dangers wrought
And the end was winning

In days of now
Armies go pow
And there is no end to war
For when battles cease
Explosives persist
Step in the wrong place and you were

THE BREAK OF DAWN

At the break of dawn
The sun comes up to shine
So we can see our fellow man
To keep them in mind

The world is an open place
Where there is room for all
That when we try to give
It is for us a place of hope

There is mine and there is the theirs
And there is all in all
If we misuse what we have
We are both in for a fall

ATTENTION SPAN

The attention span of a child is short
That of an adult too
You must be brief, concise and short
To get your message through

Make it short
Make if sweet
Your message must be concise
And oh so neat

If you would be remembered
For what you have thought
For ideas must be in a story
Or something they bought

THOSE WITHOUT LOVE

To those without love
Or hope or trust
There are things to do
Things they must

Love is divine
For those who have
To the parched soul
It is a soothing salve

If you are without love
Or hope or trust
Don't let it kill your soul
Your total person rust

For there is always hope
There is always love
It comes from within you
It comes from above

IF I HAD

If I had
If I were
If this had happened to me
I would use
I would be
I would have experienced harmony

But I have
But I am
But this has happened to me
Therefore I use
Therefore I am
Therefore it depends on me

CHANGE

Change is coming
So they say
But often we should ask
"Who are they?"

Change is the order
Of the world at large
It cannot be stopped
No matter how we charge

Change is inevitable
For all living things
Often for the better
The benefits it brings

Change is all about us
A part of our life
We can profit from it
If we can stand the strife

As surely as we live
Change will come to us
If we find when it's coming
We can use without a fuss

IN EVERY DAY

In every day
In every way
We find that we judged
By our fellow man
The work of their hands
As through life we trudge

Remember, though
What you sow
You will also reap
As life you go through
Paid back for what you do
Will not be cheap

So do not judge
How others trudge
Through this life of toil and sin
For when they try to do their best
And help all the rest
They will in the end win

WE ARE TESTED

We are tested each and every day
To see of what we are made
If we work and pass the test
We are sure to be paid

If we fail the test
Compromise who we are
It will come back to us
From good things bar

But whatever we do
We know life goes on
We will be tested again
Pass or fail and soon

HATE

Hate is an evil bug
It eats our very soul
Causing us to lose sleep
Destroying that which makes us whole

We can hate anyone
Hate with a passion
Try to give it vent
Whenever it is in fashion

When hate is given vent
When we take to action
We condemn ourselves
To a final destruction

WHAT IS LOVE

A golden ray of the sun
Shining in the water
Dark clouds in the sky
Attending to each other

An emotion so wide and deep
It launches a thousand ships
A saying so trite
It comes when the tongue slips

This is what we call love
It makes our hearts beat
It sets us glowing
And we think it's neat

But whether young or old
Whether woman or man
We search for the meaning of love
And get it when we can

SORRY ABOUT THAT

When you say,
All you can say
What do you say?
"Sorry about that"

When you know you've goofed
And your boss has he proof
What do you say?
"Sorry about that"

When there's no other way
To express what you mean
What do you say?
"Sorry about that"

It doesn't change a thing
It has a hollow ring
What do you say?
"Sorry about that"

When you can't man amends
For your many sins
What do you say?
"Sorry about that"

INCIDENT ON A ROAD

Sometimes you hear a story
Of an experience someone has had
It sounds worse than it was
Or not nearly as bad

I had a friend tell me of riding in a car
The windows down, this is a class
When someone threw out a glass bottle
And showered them with glass

I did not think it so bad
That it would not be so ill
Until it happened to me
Then I had an urge to kill

While driving in my car one day
It was hot so my windows were down
From the car in front of me
A glass bottle was thrown

The bottle hit the road
A shower of glass hit me
If the glass had flown differently
I now would not be able to see

So when you are driving
You are not all alone
You may not wish to do
Things for which you must atone

WE WALK THE WALK OF LIFE

We walk the walk of life
We do not know the end
But the question we must ask
Where do we begin?

To know the beginning
The direction we must go
Is all for us in life
All we can know

Yet the end is important
Must ever be our goal
For it makes us who we are
Determines the fate of our soul

THE LEAKY BOAT

It was but a small leak
In the bottom of the boat
Just a small ooze
Not something to note

By the by as time went by
As we looked elsewhere
The boat sank beneath the waves
It wasn't there

So it is with resources
That we use
We use but a little
But finally we lose

So what does this mean?
What can we do?
Recycle what we can
This means you

THE HUMAN CHILD

The human child is weak and frail
It cannot even hold itself
It can be pray for anything
If left without guiding help

The human child grows
Learn many things
Of right and wrong
The consequences it brings

The human child is a man
Who lives and loves
He seeks to know the way
With help from above

The human child is a woman
Who seeks to have her man
She is the mother of generations
Raises her child the best she can

The human child is old
Having lived and loved and grown
When the end does come
The earth collects its own

ITS EASY

It's easy to run up debt
As easy as living
But when the bills come due
Your creditors are not forgiving

You make a list
A list headed by "I want"
Before you take what's on the list
Consider and don't

Some debts are for money
Some are for time
On all debts you must pay interest
Far above prime

Borrowing is easy
Spending is fun
Repaying is the pits
A rough race to run

Don't take on debts of another
Settle those you own
For how you pay your debts
Will follow you home

ON BEING POLITICALLY CORRECT

Being politically correct
Is not written into law
Being politically incorrect
Your career will take a yaw

Offend no one
Whether woman, black or red
The repercussions will follow
You will wish you were dead

Guard your thoughts
Thoughts become words
You will be sorry
If your thoughts are heard

Follow what I say
Follow this advice
One misplaced word
Negates a lifetime of being nice

THE POEM IS NOT

A poem is not just a rhyme
Rhymes can be made by any fool
A poem is a thought from life
It is the philosopher's tool

Great poems speak to us
From out of our deepest soul
They speak of our victories
Of defeats lasting toll

So write poems for the ages
Write and never give up
For many ages from now
You will be in eternity's book

WHEN AT LAST

When at last the deed is done
You've done your best
You can know that the end is near
You can at last get some rest

Know the purpose of your deed
Know the end you desire
For as time goes by
Before the opportunity does expire

Know that you've done your best
To help the time of man
For this is your life
To do the best you can

Know that in times to come
People will remember all you did
In the eternal record of life
Your deeds will eternity's bid

So live your life to the full
Do not turn away
For we must be as we are
On that eternal day

AS WE TRAVEL THE ROAD OF LIFE

As we travel the road of life
We must walk alone
We may depend upon others
Who travel to their home

Always be careful whom you trust
With what you consider your own
But know that the travel is the road
That we all must travel on

We travel from our beginning to the end
We travel both fast and slow
For we meet many people along the way
Many we would like to know

So greet each day with hope
Greet each person with peace
You may help them on their way
They may go to your place

THE SPIDER

The spider spins a web
A silken thread in tow
It is a safety line
To catch it as it does go

Its web catches many things
Hapless creatures in its orb
Takes them for its own
Its lunch to be absorbed

We are not a spider
By hunger driven on
But a creature of reason
Our skills to hone

WORK IS A FOUR LETTER WORD

Work is a four letter word
That is not new
We spend our lives at it
It gives us something to do

When we have enough time
Or enough money saved
We set out for retired life
And say that we had slaved

Retirement life is new
A real change in what we do
We start at the beginning
And hope that the end is true

But in the end
It is useful that we must be
For if we are not useful
We may as well be a tree

HIT THE ROAD

Hit the road
Hit it on a run
You thought you could stay
You thought you'd have some fun

But you got caught
Doing what you ought not
Now your eternal record
Has a dark, dark spot

When you came to us
We welcomed you with open arms
But then you did this thing
Our living space did harm

Hit the road, you guy
And never come back
Hit the road, guy
Good behavior you lack

DEER IN THE FIELD

Deer in the field
Deer on the road
One looks peaceful
The other forebode

To the farmer
Both are bad
Deer in the crops
Be a hunter, be glad

For the driver
In a car
Deer in the road
Once hit, neither are

THE WISHING TREE

When I was a child
I wanted a tree
Whose fruit would come
To be a wish for me

I'd wish for things
For gold and candy and cars
But finding a wishing tree
Was not in my stars

Now I am a man
I have come to be me
But still I'd like to have
A good old wishing tree

SOME SURFACES

Some surfaces are flat
Some are round
Some set us in motion
Some get us down

As with surfaces
So it is with life
Sometimes life is stable
Sometimes filled with strife

When the outcome
Oft times depends on us
Whether we accept the facts
Or raise a fuss

The secret of life
Is not what we do
But to know the situation
It all depends on you

ABOUT THE AUTHOR

Richard Gold was born in Bartow, Florida and attended college and worked for the Government for 40 years. He has been a Christian and writing poems for as long. Gold is now retired which gives him time to continue writing. Gold lives in Indian Head, Maryland with Penny, his artistically talented wife.

www.ingramcontent.com/pod-product-compliance
Lightning Source LLC
Chambersburg PA
CBHW022341040426

42449CB00006B/659